FUNDAMENTAL CONCEPTS OF ACTUARIAL SCIENCE

CHARLES L. TROWBRIDGE, F.S.A., M.A.A.A., E.A.

CENTENNIAL EDITION

ACTUARIAL EDUCATION AND RESEARCH FUND

Expressions of Opinion

Expressions of opinion stated in this book are those of the author,
and are not the opinion or the position of the Actuarial Education
and Research Fund. The Actuarial Education and Research Fund
assumes no responsibility for statements made or opinions expressed
in this book.

ISBN 0-9623118-0-4

CONTENTS

Preface for the Actuarial Education and Research Fund

There is a natural division between fundamental actuarial concepts, the foundations which must be mastered to enter the actuarial profession, and standards, the practices which must be mastered to continue in the actuarial profession. It exists in law as the distinction between the constitution and statutory law. It exists in theology as the division between scriptures and the commentaries. It exists in taxation as the difference between statutes and regulation.

In the long run, statements on actuarial practices will be erected on principles which in turn are built on fundamental ideas and concepts. These fundamentals will be relatively invariant over time, while standards will respond to current issues facing the actuarial profession. If the standards of practice that are developed are to be consistent, such standards must be related to a coherent intellectual foundation—a set of fundamental actuarial concepts such as set out in this work.

Each segment of the actuarial profession in North America has its own practice issues. On the other hand, if actuarial standards are to be effective, they must be supported by actuaries working in all areas of specialization. To elicit this support, it is important to identify the common ideas underlying all areas of actuarial practice. This fact moved the Actuarial Standards Board (ASB) in 1987 to commission a monograph on the fundamental concepts underlying the actuarial profession.

With funding from an anonymous donor, the Actuarial Education and Research Fund (AERF) undertook the development of such a monograph and selected Charles L. Trowbridge as the author. Mr. Trowbridge is the retired Senior Vice President and Chief Actuary of The Principal Financial Group. Some of Mr. Trowbridge's other activities during his distinguished career include service as Chief Actuary of the Social Security Administration, as Professor of Actuarial Science at the University of Michigan, as Editor of *The Actuary* and as President of the Society of Actuaries.

A Monograph Project Committee was established to oversee the project. Members of that Committee were Curtis E. Huntington (Chairman), J. Gary LaRose and Charles Barry H. Watson, who were Directors of AERF and George B. Swick, who was a member of the ASB. In addition to the Committee members, several outside reviewers were enlisted to critique the monograph. These individuals were Douglas C. Borton, Phyllis A. Doran, James C. Hickman, Charles L. McClenahan and R. Stephen Radcliffe. John A. Mereu and Howard Young contributed to the development of the monograph. Finally, the AERF's Research Director, Mark G. Doherty, his Administrative Assistant, Judith Yore, and the Society of Actuaries' Research Librarian, Donna R. Richardson, also provided significant support.

As the actuarial profession celebrates its centennial in North America in 1989, the Directors of AERF are pleased to present this monograph to our fellow actuaries as well as others interested in the actuarial profession.

April 1989

Author's Preface

An author typically uses a preface to acknowledge the help of others. For this work the AERF preface does this most adequately. It is left to me to thank the AERF itself, and especially Curtis Huntington. Because I was away at a critical period earlier this year, a heavier than intended burden fell to him.

Another common use for a preface is the author's acknowledgement of responsibility for errors, omissions or other weak points. It has seemed to me that an author making such a statement is subtly claiming credit for the strong points as well. In this case, while I would like to claim overall responsibility, I cannot in good conscience do so. Too much of the thinking behind this monograph preceded my becoming involved.

The credit for this work, if in fact it proves to be successful, belongs to James C. Hickman. While the AERF is technically correct in its statement that the Actuarial Standards Board commissioned this effort, from my perspective it was Dr. Hickman, from an ASB base, who not only conceived the project, but drew up the outline which ultimately became the table of contents. In effect it was he who pointed out the path; I only walked it.

Because I found myself in full accord with Dr. Hickman's original outline, I was pleased to have been selected as the author. I hope that the actuarial profession will be equally pleased with the result.

Charles L. Trowbridge
April 1989

Chapter I

Introduction

Purpose

The purpose of this monograph is the identification and the delineation of the fundamental intellectual concepts upon which actuarial science is based. These concepts are relatively few in number, and may be well understood by the actuaries who employ them; but the actuarial profession has not previously organized these concepts into a cohesive whole.

Through the Actuarial Standards Board, and a similar effort in Canada, North American actuaries are currently engaged in the development of actuarial standards, guides to the performance of a wide range of actuarial tasks. A related effort is the development of actuarial principles, recently undertaken by the Casualty Actuarial Society and the Society of Actuaries. The profession seems to be moving toward a three-tier structure, the first level is composed of the fundamental concepts at which this monograph is aimed, and the third the standards toward which the overall effort is eventually directed. The second level includes the principles that actuaries employ, as they apply fundamental concepts to practical problems. Principles may be more specific to one kind of actuarial endeavor, and may place more emphasis on methodology, than fundamental concepts, though there may well be considerable overlap.

This monograph leaves the development of standards to the Actuarial Standards Board, the definition and statement of actuarial principles to the committees on actuarial principles, and concentrates on fundamental concepts or foundations (these two terms to be used interchangeably) of actuarial science. A sharp distinction between foundations and standards is drawn intentionally. The intellectual content that underlies all of actuarial science is in the former, while standards emphasize practice rather than theory, and are much more detailed.

Since principles and standards are built on the foundations of intellectual content, the development of the former must logically await the latter. This monograph is an attempt to put forth the foundations, as a necessary preliminary step in the successful development of standards. Standards may depend upon one or more principles as well.

This monograph is also intended as a means for emphasizing the essential unity of the actuarial profession.

Audience

This monograph is primarily addressed to those who think of themselves as professional actuaries. Since actuaries are already aware of these basic concepts, and do not need to have them elaborated, the monograph is not a textbook, nor does it go very far into actuarial mathematics.

The monograph should also be of value to those in associated disciplines and to those considering entrance into the actuarial profession. The profession is not well known and there are many misconceptions about what actuaries do. A clear statement of fundamental actuarial concepts can do much to identify the profession in the minds of others.

The primary audience, however, remains the actuarial profession. Other audiences and other purposes must be secondary.

Geographical Range

The sponsor of this monograph is the Actuarial Education and Research Fund, a North American organization devoted to education and research in actuarial science. The author is North American as well. It would be strange indeed if this work did not reflect a North American viewpoint.

However, that is not the intention. Actuarial science knows no national boundaries. It has an active international professional organization (the International Actuarial Association) that publishes papers presented at quadrennial international congresses. The intended subject of this monograph is the fundamental concepts of actuarial science as an international discipline – not actuarial science as it is practiced in North America.

Brief History of the Actuarial Profession

The actuarial profession in North America is celebrating its centennial in 1989, though actuarial science has earlier beginnings in Europe. The formal founding of the profession in North America occurred in 1889, with the formation of a professional organization then known as the Actuarial Society of America.

That Society had its roots in Great Britain, and was modeled after two earlier actuarial organizations, the Institute of Actuaries (formed in London in 1848) and the Faculty of Actuaries (formed in Edinburgh in 1856). The Actuarial Society of America, copying its British predecessors, published a professional journal, held periodic meetings, and attempted to be a truly professional organization.

In 1909, a second and somewhat competing North American actuarial organization, the American Institute of Actuaries, reflecting western and smaller insurance company interests, was formed. In 1949, the Society and the Institute merged to become the present Society of Actuaries.

Before the merger, another actuarial organization came into existence. In 1914, the Casualty Actuarial Society (CAS) was founded by actuaries engaged in the development of the newly emerging workers' compensation plans. Soon thereafter, the CAS became the professional body for actuaries specializing in property/casualty insurance.

The Conference of Actuaries in Public Practice was formed in 1950 to meet the needs of consulting actuaries and others employed outside of the insurance industry.

The mid-1960s saw the formation of the American Academy of Actuaries and the Canadian Institute of Actuaries, both intended to represent the profession in dealings with government and with the general public. At about the same time, a group particularly interested in smaller pension plans (actuaries and administrators) formed the American Society of Pension Actuaries.

This rather complex structure of actuarial organizations should not obscure the essential unity of actuarial thought. Although the profession in North America appears to have life and casualty branches, and some specialization by type or nation of employment, the intellectual foundations are essentially the same.

Evolution

In earlier days, most of those who thought of themselves as actuaries were employees of life insurance companies and hence part of the insurance industry. The few consulting actuaries providing actuarial services to the smaller companies were closely associated with the industry. This close connection between the actuarial profession and the insurance industry is largely a thing of the past.

Actuaries today are importantly engaged in work for property/casualty companies, as well as life insurance companies and health organizations. Many are consulting actuaries working with sponsors of employee benefit plans; others are employed by government and by academia. Classification of actuaries by vocational endeavor is no longer very meaningful, and is not important to the purposes of this monograph.

As actuarial endeavor has evolved it has become more complex and actuarial science, like other professional disciplines, has become more specialized. The Society of Actuaries has created specialized Sections within the overall Society structure. Actuaries specializing in casualty insurance and in public practice have maintained their distinct organizations. Actuaries share the same fundamental concepts, however, so this monograph is intended for all.

Readers should understand that many (if not most) of the fundamental concepts of actuarial science pre-date the formation of the actuarial profession in North America. These ideas are indeed so fundamental that they can be traced to a time long before the actuarial profession developed anywhere. The intellectual history of each of these basic ideas, to the extent that this history can now be unearthed, will be touched upon in later chapters. We will find that some of these concepts, originally only crudely expressed ideas, have evolved into disciplined mathematical models.

Following Chapters

Each of the next seven chapters will set forth an idea, or a cluster of related ideas, fundamental to actuarial science, and hence a part of its foundations. It will be found that some of these concepts are basically mathematical, while others are taken from economics, psychology or philosophy. The order of presentation appears logical to the author, but no implication that one concept or idea is more essential than another is intended.

Illustrations will be included for the purpose of understanding, and to show the breadth of matters with which actuaries are involved, but have no further significance. None of the illustrations is, in itself, a foundation. Each of these chapters will conclude with a short list of references, selected to give the reader further insight into the concepts of that chapter.

The final chapter discusses the role of fundamental concepts in the development of standards, and discusses the ways that conflicts may be resolved.

Chapter II

Economics of Risk

Utilitarianism as a philosophy, and risk aversion as a feature of human psychology, lead to the evolution of financial security systems as a means of reducing the financial consequences of unfavorable events. Actuaries are those with a deep understanding of financial security systems, their reasons for being, their complexity, their mathematics, and the way they work.

Introduction

The word "risk" used as a noun expresses the possibility of loss or injury. As a verb, the same word denotes the exposing of one's person or property to loss or injury. Within the common meaning of "risk," there are thus two distinct elements, the idea of loss or injury, and that of uncertainty.

In the economic setting within which actuaries work, loss is usually expressed in monetary terms. Theft, embezzlement, and adverse court judgments cause loss of wealth, and are direct forms of economic loss. Death, disability, retirement, and unemployment are various forms of income loss. Damage to property impairs the value of that property, where value is a measure of the ability of a property to produce a flow of desired goods and services. In short, the loss or injury is often measurable in monetary units. When it is, we use the term "economic loss."

Though economic loss is seldom certain, neither is it impossible. If the probability of economic loss is greater than zero but less than one, some party is exposed to the possibility of economic loss. We here define this exposure as economic risk. When applied to financial markets, this concept of risk is essentially the same as the "down-side" risk in stocks or bonds, but it is different from another use of the word "risk," denoting any uncertainty as to market behavior.

It is almost axiomatic that human beings have an aversion to economic loss, and hence to economic risk. Some persons are more risk averse than others, but few expose themselves or their belongings needlessly. There are a few individuals who seem to thrive on taking chances, even though there seems to be no possibility of gain; but even these must find some satisfaction that compensates for the possibility of negative economic consequences.

Avoidance or Mitigation of Economic Risk

Human beings have been reasonably successful in developing means by which risk can be reduced. In order to reduce risk to the person we have police protection, self-defense techniques, rescue organizations, safety equipment, etc. To protect property we use fire departments, smoke or burglar alarms, security systems, and building codes. The technology for making person and property more secure is impressive. The lowering of the probability that an adverse event will take place, or the lowering of the damage when such an event does occur, is the first order of defense against any loss; and economic loss is no exception.

There remain, however, many forms of economic loss that cannot be prevented. There are limits below which the probability of economic loss or the degree of damage cannot be reduced, even when the first order defense mechanisms are most successful. Recognizing these limits, modern society has developed ways to cope with the financial consequences of economic risk, even though the risk itself cannot be avoided. For the purposes of this monograph we will use the term "financial security systems" to describe these methods. The actuary has a special relationship to these systems. The existence and significance of this relationship is one of the foundations upon which actuarial science is built.

Financial Security Systems

Financial security systems make use of the principle that risk averse individuals will often prefer to take a small but certain loss in preference to a large uncertain one. Where economic loss cannot be avoided, it can often be shared. The pooling of economic risk, resulting in a small loss to many rather than a large loss to the unfortunate few, is the basic idea. For the purposes of this monograph, we define a financial security system as any economic system designed primarily to transfer economic risk from the individual to an aggregate or collective of individuals, or from one collective to another.

The words insurance and assurance have, for many, a similar connotation. In this monograph, we consider most insurance systems as financial security systems, but not all financial security systems as insurance. The more general term includes systems that are not generally thought of as insurance (e.g., pension plans, HMOs, public welfare systems), those that are arguably insurance (social security), and some of those arrangements called "self-insurance."

Classification of Financial Security Systems

Financial security systems can be classified by the type of economic loss that they are intended to minimize. Plans intended to replace loss of a worker's income include life insurance, disability insurance, unemployment insurance, workers' compensation, and retirement plans. Property insurance reduces the financial impact of natural hazards—fire, wind, earthquake, or flood—or man-caused events such as vandalism or theft. Health insurance in its several forms pays much of the unbudgetable medical and dental expense, while liability insurance offers protection against a determination of legal liability.

Financial security systems can be voluntary, compulsory, or somewhere between. They may be within the private sector or a part of government. They may or may not be closely related to employment—i.e., part of the salary/wage package. They may be wide ranging plans that affect many, or narrow and small plans that pertain to only a few. While many financial security systems are designed to reduce the economic risk of individuals, some perform a similar role for business enterprises, for non-profit organizations, or for government. Organizations of people, as well as individuals, are risk averse. Even insurance companies, specifically organized to assume risks of individuals, must make careful provision, through reinsurance or otherwise, for their own economic risk.

Financial Security Systems as Transfer Mechanisms

Financial security systems can also be viewed as transfer mechanisms, whereby money is transferred from one group or class of persons to another. Transfers, from the many for whom the insured-against-event did not occur to the few for whom it did, are at the very heart of financial security systems.

Financial security systems also employ some secondary transfers. Employee benefit plans make use of an "employer" transfer, essentially as part of the system by which employees are compensated for the work they perform. The social security system relies upon an "intergeneration" transfer. Some financial security systems, particularly those of government under a public welfare rationale, are "subsidies" of one group of persons by another. Such systems are not included within the common understanding of insurance. However, we include systems which employ secondary transfers here because they fit the definition we have chosen for financial security systems.

Outside of our definition are those financial institutions that make it easier for an individual to save or to diversify, and hence to reduce economic risk; but that do not involve a significant transfer from the individual to a collective. Thrift institutions and mutual funds, although they have some financial security characteristics, are not in themselves financial security systems, as the term is used in this monograph. Systems serving the financial markets that do meet our definition are those that guarantee the investor's principal via a transfer of risk to a collective.

The Philosophic Base – Utilitarianism

Most modern economic systems, be they capitalistic or socialistic, rest on the philosophic principle of utilitarianism, very roughly stated as the greatest good for the greatest number over the longest period of time. Financial security systems rest on this same base.

The classical philosophical utilitarians were Jeremy Bentham and John Stuart Mill, writing in Britain during the nineteenth century. Perhaps a majority of more recent philosophers espouse some form of the same utilitarian concept, and it is clearly the principle underlying much of modern western society. Whether the good that utilitarians attempt to maximize is called "happiness," "pleasure," or "utility," and whether the maximization is individual or collective, are areas of controversy, but the general principle seems well accepted.

Utility Theory and Risk Aversion

Given a set of axioms for coherence among preferences, one can prove the existence of a real number utility function, defined on the set of states in the world and maintaining the individual's preference ordering. An important part of modern utility theory is that a person's expected utility for uncertain future wealth is something akin, but not identical to, the expected values of future wealth. People tend not to be indifferent between a large but uncertain loss, and a small but certain loss – generally preferring the latter. Risk aversion, primarily a psychological phenomenon, is a part of utilitarianism, and hence a part of the rationale behind modern financial security systems.

The Actuarial Role

Just as economic systems are the realm of the economist, social systems are the realm of the sociologist, and electrical systems are the realm of the electrical engineer, financial security systems have become the realm of the actuary. The uniqueness of the actuarial profession lies in the actuary's understanding of financial security systems in general, and the inner workings of the many different types in particular. The role of the actuary is that of the designer, the adaptor, the problem solver, the risk estimator, the innovator, and the technician of the continually changing field of financial security systems.

The actuarial profession understands, however, that the actuary's role is not exclusive. Many others, professionals or otherwise, play an important role in financial security systems. Among these are economists, accountants, lawyers, sociologists, politicians, administrators, regulators, marketers — to name only a few. Actuarial skills must mesh with the capabilities of others if financial security systems are to be successful in minimizing the financial consequences of economic risk.

There are, moreover, some systems that fit our definition where the actuary has, at least in the past, had little impact. This may be especially true for government systems in the public assistance or welfare area, and for systems associated with financial markets. Even some of the systems which have the word "insurance" in their name, the FHA's mortgage insurance, the Federal Deposit Insurance Corporation (FDIC), and the unemployment insurance systems of the United States and Canada, operate largely without actuarial help.

Summary

Utilitarianism as a philosophy, and risk aversion as a feature of human psychology, lead to the evolution of financial security systems as a means of reducing the financial consequences of unfavorable events. Actuaries are those professionals with a deep understanding of, and training in, financial security systems; their reason for being, their complexity, their mathematics, and the way they work.

References

Utilitarianism
Albee, Ernest. *The Beginnings of English Utilitarianism*. Boston: Ginn and Company, 1897.

Mill, John S. *Utilitarianism*. London: Parker, son, and Bourn, 1863.

Rawls, John. *A Theory of Justice*. Cambridge: Belknap Press, Harvard University Press, 1971.

Utility Theory
Borch, Karl H. *The Economics of Uncertainty*. Princeton, N.J.: Princeton University Press, 1968.

Bowers, Newton L., Jr., Hans U. Gerber, James C. Hickman, Donald A. Jones, and Cecil J. Nesbitt. "The Economics of Insurance." Chapter 1 in *Actuarial Mathematics*. Itasca, Ill.: Society of Actuaries, 1986.

Friedman, Milton, and L. J. Savage. "The Utility Analysis of Choices Involving Risk." *Journal of Political Economy* 56(August, 1948): 270-304.

Financial Security Systems As Transfer Mechanisms
Trowbridge, C.L. "Insurance as a Transfer Mechanism." *Journal of Risk and Insurance* 42(1975): 1-15.

Chapter III

Random Variables

The impossibility of certainty is one of the facts with which all humans contend. The study of random variables, known also as probability and statistics, is helpful to humans in dealing with uncertainty. Probability and statistics provide many of the ideas on which financial security systems, aiming at reducing human uncertainty, depend.

Introduction

The foundations of the theory of probability lie in the seventeenth and eighteenth centuries when Bernouli, Gauss, LaPlace, and other mathematicians began the study of what have come to be known as random variables.

A single throw of a cubical die can have six possible outcomes. The variable, the number of pips on the upper face when the die comes to rest, can take the values 1, 2, 3, 4, 5, or 6. The physical properties of the die suggest that the six possible results are equally likely. This supposition can be confirmed by recording the results of a large number of throws, and finding that the proportion of times that each result occurs is approximately 1/6. This line of inquiry leads to the statement that the probability of getting any specific result when a fair die is cast is 1/6.

The early study of probability emphasized games of chance, where the number of possible outcomes, though sometimes large, is clearly finite, and the physical characteristics of the cards, coins, or dice give strong clues to the evaluation of the underlying probabilities. Later the concept was extended to continuous variables, and to those where probabilities must be obtained empirically, via experiment or observation.

As an example of a continuous random variable whose distribution must be investigated by direct observation, consider the measurement of the individual heights of the population of adult American males. A priori, we may expect any result along the continuous line from under 60 inches to more than 80. If we actually measure the heights of a random sample of 100, and we find 13 whose height falls between 70 and 72 inches, we can say that our estimate of the probability that an American man, selected at random, has a height within this range is 13%. We must view this result as only an estimate, however, because we realize that if the experiment were to be repeated on several different selections of 100 subjects, the results might be different. Not only may accurate measurements vary from sample to sample, but there may well be some error in measurement (or in the recording thereof). We must also consider whether our sample is truly random, whether it is large enough to be statistically significant, and whether there may be problems with independence.

The concept of a probability distribution leads directly to the concept of an average or arithmetic mean. A mean of a random variable is a weighted average of all possible numerical values, using the associated probabilities as weights. The mean result of the throw of a cubical die must be $1/6 (1+2+3+4+5+6) = 3.5$, if the six possible results are equally likely, and the probability of each is thus 1/6. For the height experiment, an estimate of the mean or average height can be obtained more directly by adding the observations and dividing by 100.

The mean or expected value of a random variable is important information, giving a good idea of the center of the distribution of probability. The variance of a probability distribution, the second moment of the distribution around the mean, is also important, giving an indication of how widely the variable is scattered.

There is much more to the study of probability and statistics than can even be suggested here. Suffice it to say that the actuary studies these related subjects in some depth, and applies the basic concepts in his daily work. The types of random variables which he encounters most frequently are the main subject of the remainder of this chapter.

"Time until Termination" Random Variables

There is a type or kind of random variable where the variable is the length of time (in seconds, hours, days, or years) that some well-defined status exists. Quality control experts study the varying length of time before a light bulb burns out, or the shelf-life of grocery products. Chemical engineers may investigate how long a paint will protect steel from rust. The medical profession is concerned with the varying amount of time between an exposure to a disease and its manifestation through physical symptoms. Actuaries study the random variables associated with the remaining length of human life, the length of a period of disability or employment, or the time between the occurrence of a claim event and its eventual settlement.

It is typical of this class of random variables that the variable length of time can be studied via a transformation into another variable q, where q is the probability that the status will terminate within a specific time period. Generally speaking, q is not constant, depending upon some time related variable (such as age or length of service). The complement of q, $1-q$, is often designated as p, and represents the probability that the status will persist to the end of the time period. In some applications the time period is reduced to an infinitesimal, and the analysis involves the study of conditional momentary probability densities, or "forces," of status termination.

A mathematical model representing T_x, the varying length of human life after the attainment of some status x, is widely used by actuaries working with life insurance, disability programs, or pension plans. This model is often referred to as a "mortality table," or less commonly, as a "life table." In its usual form, the table displays l_{x+t}, the number of persons alive at age x assumed to be still alive at age $x+t$, where t takes all integral values from 1 to some high age at which the number living is assumed to be 0. Subtraction of any l_{x+t} from the preceding l_{x+t-1} shows the number assumed to die between age $x+t-1$ and age $x+t$, and hence one form of the probability distribution of T_x.

A similar, though somewhat more complicated, model is commonly used by pension actuaries in connection with employer sponsored pension plans. Here the variable of interest is the remaining length of service of an employee hired t years ago at age x, and hence age $x+t$ today. This "service table" model differs from the mortality table in that discontinuance of an employee's service can be caused by other factors than death—employee withdrawal (voluntary or involuntary), retirement, or disability. A table that recognizes more than one way in which a status may be terminated is known as a "multiple decrement" table. The multiple decrement concept is also useful in the analysis of disability coverages.

"Number of Claims" Random Variables

A second class of random variables with which actuaries are especially associated is the number of claims arising within a given time period from a specified block of insurance. Since the number of policies or certificates from which claims may arise is rarely constant, the random variable may be better expressed as the "frequency rate," defined as the number of claims per unit exposed. The frequency rate may be expected to vary from one time period to another, for any of several reasons, including that of statistical fluctuation. Some types of insurance exhibit seasonal variation, and others may have a long-term trend. Frequency rates can also be expressed as momentary or continuous "forces," permitting the use of calculus in the mathematical analysis.

This variable recognizes the possibility of multiple claims from a single insured within the exposure period. It is thus a more appropriate model for the study of insurances (e.g., health insurance) that have these characteristics than the time until termination model often used in life insurance. For several reasons, the assumptions behind the binomial, negative binomial, and Poisson claim count processes seem to be reasonable models for claim frequency studies, so these probability distributions are widely used.

"Claim Amount" Random Variables

Except in those few types of insurance where the dollar amount of each claim is specified by the insurance contract, another variable of great actuarial interest is the dollar amount of the claim, given that a claim event has occurred. For many coverages the range of possible claim amounts is very wide, from as little as $1 to as much as the maximum coverage provided. Claim amount variables (often described as intensity or severity) tend not to cluster around the mean, and hence to exhibit high variances. For many kinds of insurance, the distribution of claim amounts is not symmetric, characteristically having a heavy tail and considerable skewness.

A study of the characteristics of the claim amount variable, as exhibited by many kinds of insurance coverage, is an important actuarial responsibility. Property/casualty actuaries, and those specializing in health insurance, are the most concerned with the variation in claim amount.

"Total Claims" Random Variables

The dollars of claims arising from a block of policies within a time period is the product of the number exposed, the claim rate experienced, and the average amount of claims. If the claim amount distributions are mutually independent and identically distributed, and do not depend upon the number of claims, then the expected value of total claims is the product of the expected number of claims and the expected claim amount. Total claims (or aggregate loss) is thus another random variable in which actuaries must be interested. Its main application is in the study of the risks to which an insurer, rather than the insured, is subject. The distribution of total claims is important to aggregate risk theory, ruin theory, and stop-loss reinsurance.

Aggregate risk theory, the study of the distribution of total claims from a given exposure, has become one of the more complex actuarial specialties. At least two mathematical models have been developed, one known as the individual risk model, the other the collective model. Both depend heavily on high speed computers to derive most practical results. Simulation is another computer-aided approach to aggregate risk theory.

The Rate of Interest as a Random Variable

Of great importance to the actuary is the rate of interest (or more generally, the rate of investment return). Interest rates vary in many dimensions, from time to time, from place to place, by degree of security risk, and by time to maturity. Financial security systems are especially sensitive to the variation of interest rates over time, so actuaries must be interested in the probability distributions, the means and variances, of a specified interest rate as it varies over time.

Historically, actuaries have used deterministic models in their treatment of the time value of money, but not because they were unaware of interest rate variation. Many of the discussions at actuarial gatherings over the years have centered around the prospects for interest rate rise or fall. The difficulty has not been a lack of concern, but rather a lack of knowledge as to the complexities of interest rate variation. North American actuaries have perhaps done less toward adding to this knowledge than European actuaries, or than some researchers in economics or finance; but if so, the situation is changing. The development of computers has opened up a range of techniques whereby interest rate variation can be modeled. It appears that this is a direction in which actuarial interest and knowledge may be expected to grow.

The Importance of Expected Values

The expected value of any random variable is the first moment or mean. Ideally the actuary works with large samples, and can be reasonably confident that the mean of his sample is a good estimate of the mean of the entire population; but the practical situation is often different.

Historically, the actuary has used expected values as the best, if not the only, measure of the magnitude of a random variable, and he has largely ignored the second and higher moments. Many of the more common actuarial calculations are deterministic rather than stochastic, based essentially on expected values. An important function that actuaries perform is estimating the means of probability distributions, using the best available data. (Only very recently have actuarial textbooks emphasized the variances of functions based upon a mortality table.)

Claim amount and total claim variables are the important exceptions to the preceding paragraph. Where probability distributions are not symmetric, large second and third moments (variance and skewness) must be considered in business decisions because of the likelihood of results differing markedly from those expected. Property/casualty and health actuaries, particularly, must deal with these difficult distributions.

Actuarial Interest in Human Mortality

Life and pension actuaries have always had an especial interest in the development and construction of mortality tables. The very earliest of such tables seems to have been the work of Edmund Halley, a noted mathematician but perhaps better known as an astronomer, who in 1693 published what has come to be known as the Breslau Table, based on records of births and deaths in a European city of that name. Among the many such tables that have been devised since, the first major one based on North American insurance data is the American Experience Table, published in 1868.

A satisfactory mortality study requires the collection of a large amount of data, usually from the records of life insurance companies, or from government death records combined with the periodic census. The methods through which mortality data can be compiled is one of the subjects that life actuaries study. Another is the means by which raw data can be "graduated," to introduce a desirable smoothness into the final product, while still preserving the basic characteristics of the observations.

Life actuaries have also been interested in the search for a mathematical formula expressing the force of mortality. The earliest of these was suggested by de Moivre in 1729. A formula proposed by Gompertz in 1825, and an extension thereof suggested by Makeham 35 years later, have been the most widely used.

The Concept of Credibility

Almost from the time that their professional organization was formed in the second decade of the twentieth century, casualty actuaries have devoted time and effort to the concept of credibility. Credibility is closely related to the problem of how to make the best interpretation of claim experience when a subsection of a population exhibits a different claim experience than the whole.

Suppose that the best a priori estimate of a claim parameter (frequency, severity, or their product) is f_1, based upon a previous study of a large exposure; but that a newly investigated subsection shows a higher or lower claim parameter, f_2. The difference, $f_1 - f_2$, may be attributed to statistical fluctuation (and hence the best estimate remains as f_1); or to real differences in the risk characteristics (in which case f_2 is presumably the better estimate for the subsection). The "credibility factor" (usually expressed as Z) is the weight $0 \leq Z \leq 1$ that one assigns to f_2, with the complementary weight, $(1-Z)$, assigned to f_1. The analytical as well as the practical problem is the best determination of Z.

It has long been recognized that Z must be an increasing function of P, where P is the subsection exposure. If P is very small,

Z should be close to 0, but as P becomes very large, Z should approach 1. The simple formula $Z = P/P+K$, where K for a specific coverage is a constant, has the above characteristics, and has been widely used ever since it was suggested for workmens' compensation by a Casualty Actuarial Society committee in 1918. Other mathematical forms have developed since.

Credibility theory has much in common with the later developing Bayesian view of statistics. Under both, prior knowledge is allowed to influence the statistical inference. The development of credibility concepts, largely by casualty actuaries, is one of the great contributions to actuarial science. Life actuaries have "borrowed" these concepts for use in the experience rating of group life, health, and even annuity coverages.

Summary

Probability and statistics, the study of random variables, is clearly one of the foundations upon which actuarial science is built. The impossibility of certainty is one of the facts with which all humans contend. In many situations the actuary's role is to help society, via financial security systems, to deal with uncertainty. Probability and statistics provide many of the tools on which such systems depend.

There are several types of random variables of especial interest to actuaries. Life and pension actuaries have more occasion to work with the "time until termination" type, while health and casualty actuaries have more direct involvement with frequency and claim amount variables. Life actuaries are necessarily students of human mortality, while casualty actuaries have a special interest in credibility.

References

Probability and Statistics

Cramer, Harald. *On the Mathematical Theory of Risk*, 1930. Reprint. Fort Wayne, Ind.: Fort Wayne Microfilms, Inc., 1959.

Feller, William. *An Introduction to Probability Theory and Its Applications*, Vol.1, 3d ed., Vol.2, 2d ed. New York: John Wiley and Sons, 1968 and 1966.

Savage, Leonard J. *The Foundation of Statistics*. 1954. rev. and enl. New York: Dover Publications, 1972.

Stigler, Stephen M. *A History of Statistics*. Cambridge: Harvard University Press, 1986.

Time until Termination

Elandt-Johnson, Regina C. and Norman L. Johnson. *Survival Models and Data Analysis*. New York: John Wiley and Sons, 1980.

Claim Frequency

Simon, LeRoy J. "The Negative Binomial and the Poisson Distributions Compared." *Proceedings of the Casualty Actuarial Society* 48(1960): 20-24.

Claim Amounts

Hogg, Robert V. and Stuart A. Klugman. *Loss Distributions*. New York: John Wiley and Sons, 1984.

Aggregate Risk Theory

Beard, Robert E., Teivo Pentikainen and Erkki Pesonen. *Risk Theory*. London: Chapman and Hall, 1977.

Bowers, Newton L., Jr., Hans U. Gerber, James C. Hickman, Donald A. Jones, and Cecil J. Nesbitt. Chapters 2, 11, 12, and 13 in *Actuarial Mathematics*. Itasca, Ill.: Society of Actuaries, 1986.

Buhlmann, Hans. *Mathematical Methods in Risk Theory.* Berlin: Springer, 1970.

Gerber, Hans U. *An Introduction to Mathematical Risk Theory.* Huebner Foundation, Monograph no. 8. Homewood, Ill.: Richard D. Irwin, 1979.

Panjer, Harry H. "The Aggregate Claims Distribution and Stop-Loss Reinsurance." *Transactions of the Society of Actuaries* 32(1980): 523-545.

Interest Rate Variation
Bellhouse, David R. and Harry H. Panjer. "Stochastic Modelling of Interest Rates with Applications to Life Contingencies." *Journal of Risk Insurance* 48(1981): 628-637.

Mortality Tables
Batten, Robert W. *Mortality Table Construction.* Englewood Cliffs, NJ: Prentice Hall, Inc., 1978.

Woolhouse, W.S.B. "On the Construction of Tables of Mortality." *Journal of the Institute of Actuaries* 13(1867): 75-102.

Credibility
Longley-Cook, Lawrence H. "An Introduction to Credibility Theory." *Proceedings of the Casualty Actuarial Society* 49(1962): 194-221.

Mayerson, Allen L. "A Bayesian View of Credibility." *Proceedings of the Casualty Actuarial Society* 51(1964): 85-104.

Rodermund, Matthew. "Preface" in *Foundations of Casualty Actuarial Science.* New York: Casualty Actuarial Society, forthcoming.

Chapter IV

The Time Value of Money

The time value of money is an important concept throughout the business and financial world, and hence a fundamental concept of actuarial science. Actuaries use this concept, together with the concept of probability, in the calculation of actuarial present values; which in turn become the building blocks in the development of actuarial models.

Introduction

A concept very close to the foundations of actuarial thought is often referred to as the "time value of money." It seems obvious to economists and businessmen of the modern commercial and industrial world that money today is "worth" more than the same amount some time hence. The price for this additional value is "interest;" or perhaps it may be viewed as "rent" (for the use of money), or "investment return." Many practical applications arise because money is so widely borrowed, lent, or invested for profit.

The theory of interest is still evolving, and is clearly a product of time and place. The charging of interest (and hence its very existence) was once barred as "usury" under Christian canon law, and is still unacceptable in much of the Islamic world. Whether interest exists in a socialistic (Marxist) state is still a matter of controversy.

The modern version of interest theory has its roots in the nineteenth century. It attempts to explain what interest is, why it has existed for most of recorded history, and the influences determining the "interest rate." It is quite clear that interest rates, as well as other measures of the time value of money, vary widely over time, place, and circumstance. Why and how they vary is a matter of considerable importance.

This chapter will not attempt a comprehensive description of the various theories as to why interest exists, but it will outline the two best accepted sub-theories. The first of these will be referred to as "time preference;" the second as "productivity of capital."

Time Preference

In large measure, the time value of money arises from the natural human preference for present goods over future goods. Since dollars and goods are interchangeable, dollars today are generally preferable to an equal amount of dollars tomorrow.

Dollars today can make the present more enjoyable (or less onerous), can raise the standard of living (or reduce the necessity for work), can be exchanged for present goods or present services, or can be employed for purposes of the future. Dollars tomorrow have only the last of these desirable attributes. Future dollars satisfy present needs only if they can be pledged, borrowed against, or otherwise moved from the future into the present.

Persons who see their present incomes as insufficient but rising, or their present expenditures as excessive but falling, have good reason to bring future income into the present, and may be expected to do so via consumer credit or other borrowing. Others, with less reason, may be profligate or impatient, unwilling to put off enjoyment until the money is at hand. In either case the preference for present dollars is strong enough that the premium for present dollars, the interest, is readily (though not always willingly) paid.

There are others of the opposite bent, who emphasize the needs of the future, provide for the rainy day, and defer income until a time when they, or their heirs, may need it more. But even these financial conservatives prefer present to future dollars, if only because money is durable and can so easily be moved into the future. For such persons, however, the preference is overcome if the inducement, once again the interest, is sufficient.

Productivity of Capital

The strong preference for present money may be adequate in itself to explain consumer borrowing and consumer lending. It also is the basic reason why people borrow to finance homes or to purchase automobiles. There is another dimension, however, to loans for business purposes. Businesses large or small require capital goods if they are to prosper. A retailer cannot sell merchandise he does not have. A farmer must plant and cultivate a crop before he can bring it to market. The retailer's place of business and inventory, and the farmer's seed, fertilizer, and machinery represent the capital goods which, combined with labor, produce business income.

In the long run, a business will be successful only if the return on the capital employed is greater than the rate of interest. That capital used in business is productive, that it can be employed to earn more capital at a rate higher than the cost of borrowing, is the justification for business borrowing and lending. The business borrower acquires the funds he needs, uses these funds to pay interest, to retire debt, and to earn his own living. Lenders too find their capital productive – their funds have grown at interest.

Productivity of capital, though it offers a somewhat different explanation of the time value of money, is by no means a theory competing with that of human time preference. These two rationales augment and strengthen one another. A successful business enterprise, already using capital and already producing income, sees an opportunity to expand and add to future income; but realizes that additional capital will be required, and that the fruits thereof will be delayed. Even if the entrepreneur has the wherewithal to make the additional investment from his own resources, his time preferences may be otherwise. The resulting business loan can be attributed to the productivity of capital and/or time preference.

When productivity of capital is taken into consideration, the time value of money takes on a meaning more general than interest alone. The time value of money is often measured by the income that capital can produce, including business profits, dividends on common stock, and other forms of investment income not directly related to debt. More generally, even idle money has a time value, in this case associated with an "opportunity" cost, the "cost" of holding money idle.

The Uncertain Future

A third aspect of the time value of money lies in the uncertainty of the future. Time preferences are affected by inability to see the future clearly. Humans tend to be risk averse, and to fear what they cannot predict. Those with a propensity to spend can easily rationalize present spending by imagining ways in which money may lose its value. Those with a tendency to save may be concerned about the safety of their invested funds, or about the future purchasing power of income deferred.

Business lending is also affected by the matter of uncertainty. Lenders require adequate security, or raise the interest rate, to reflect the risk that the loan may not be repaid, or that the loan will be repaid in depreciated dollars.

Whether future uncertainties are a third rationale for the time value of money, or are better viewed as an influence affecting the measure or the magnitude of this time value, may be unimportant. Interest rates can be expected to rise when uncertainty is high. Fears of inflation, the possibility of war, worries about trade deficits or the value of the currency, are all conducive to increased uncertainty, and to a higher price for present dollars.

The Level of Interest Rates

The foregoing may be an adequate explanation as to why a positive interest rate exists, but it has little to say about what that interest rate may be, and why and how it varies from time to time and from place to place. For an analysis of interest rate behavior, monetary considerations must be taken into account.

It is commonly held that the price of money, like the price of other goods, varies with supply and demand. At least in theory, and if all other factors are held constant, the prevailing interest rate at any point in time is that rate at which the supply and demand for loanable funds come into balance, and the money market "clears." The supply of money, to some extent controlled by the policies of the central bank, clearly has an influence, as do expectations of inflation.

In any case, there is no single rate of interest, even at a specified time and place. Interest rates reflect the length of time for which money is lent, the credit of the borrower, legal restrictions, custom, and certain market rigidities. There is usually a spread between the rate an individual can earn on his savings and the rate he must pay when he borrows, so an individual may have different "time values" depending on whether he is a borrower or a lender.

Predictions of the course of any interest rate, even as to its general direction, are fraught with difficulty. Even when made by the so-called experts, such predictions seem to be wrong as often as they are right. Moreover, such predictions are often limited to the short term or the near future, and hence are of limited use for the analysis of the expected behavior of long term financial systems.

The Actuary's Relationship to the Time Value of Money

Clearly, any uniqueness that the actuarial profession may claim cannot be based on any special knowledge of the time value of money. Like any person involved in business, economics, or finance, the actuary uses the time value concept in his daily work; but the same can be said for many of those employed in business affairs.

Even so, the actuary's interest in the time value of money is somewhat more intense, and his knowledge based on a deeper understanding, than the interest and knowledge of the typical informed business person. There may be two reasons for the special relationship that actuaries feel with the interest concept.

First, the actuary comes from a background of mathematics. The requirements of his professional training cause the actuary to become especially skilled in the mathematics of finance. A high proportion of the textbooks in this branch of applied mathematics, some of them dating back to the turn of the century, were written by and for actuaries. Many of the tables compiled for the easy solution of practical interest problems were first made up by actuaries, though these same tables have been widely used by others. The references include a selection from a long series of texts in the mathematics of finance that one generation of actuaries, or another, has studied.

Second, and of more importance, the financial systems that make up the particular field of study of the actuarial profession tend to be those with a long time horizon, and hence those where the time value of money makes a real difference. Even the typical short-term insurance contract is often renewed, and becomes in effect a mid-to-long term arrangement. Contrasting the span of time inherent in a life insurance policy or an employee retirement plan with the much shorter time period of commercial banking or consumer lending, one can readily appreciate the actuary's emphasis on the time value of money. The actuary makes no claim as to any special ability to predict interest rates. He does, however, appreciate the power of compound interest, and knows how to apply its mathematics to the solution of practical business problems.

The profession makes very wide use of the concept of "present value," in which money flows are "discounted"–i.e., valued in a current time frame by taking into explicit account the time value of money. The basic formula for the present value of a dollar t years hence is $(1+i)^{-t}$, where i is the effective annual rate of interest. Present values, often involving discounts for other factors as well but invariably recognizing the time value of money, are among the most important tools that actuaries use. That others use these same tools, albeit less explicitly or less consistently, is of little importance. It is important that the present value concept has met the test of time, and that it continues to be one of the most basic ideas upon which actuaries, among others, depend.

The inexperienced actuary may tend to take an assumption about the time value of money as a given, and devote little or no attention to the appropriateness of the interest rate assumed. As he gains knowledge and experience, however, the actuary learns to differentiate between gross interest and net, before tax and after tax, nominal, effective, and "real" rates of interest, and internal rates of return. He gains a knowledge of the yield curve, the relationships between interest rates for different maturity periods. He recognizes that any specific interest rate has a basic component for time preference, and additional components for the possibility of default and the expectation of inflation. He knows that interest rate changes can affect assets and liabilities differently.

Summary

The concept of the time value of money is important to actuarial science, and to other areas of the economic world. Actuaries use this concept, together with the concept of random variability, in the calculation of actuarial present values. Present values allow actuaries to make judgments as to actuarial equivalence, and other matters important to the profession.

References

The Theory of Interest
Boehm-Bawerk, Eugen Von. *Capital and Interest*. 3 Vols. 1884–1909. Translated by Hans F. Sennholz and George D. Huncke. Spring Mills, Penn.: Libertarian Press, 1959.

Cassel, Gustave. *The Nature and Necessity of Interest*. 1903. Reprint. New York: Augustus M. Kelley Publishers, 1971.

Conard, Joseph. *An Introduction to the Theory of Interest*. Berkeley: University of California, 1959.

Fisher, Irving. *The Theory of Interest*. 1930. Reprint. New York: Augustus M. Kelley Publishers, 1986.

Mathematics of Finance
Butcher, Marjorie V. and Cecil J. Nesbitt. *Mathematics of Compound Interest*. Ann Arbor, Mich.: Ulrich, 1971.

Donald, D. W. *Compound Interest and Annuities-certain*. London: Heinemann, 1975.

Kellison, Stephen G. *The Theory of Interest*. Homewood, Ill.: Richard D. Irwin Inc., 1970.

McCutcheon, J. J. and W. F. Scott. *An Introduction to the Mathematics of Finance*. London: Heinemann, 1986.

Todhunter, Ralph. *The Institute of Actuaries' Textbook on Compound Interest and Annuities-certain*. 3d ed. rev. and enl. Ulrich, by R.C. Simmonds and T.P. Thompson. Cambridge: Institute of Actuaries, 1931.

Chapter V

Individual Model

Actuaries have developed a generalized mathematical model for the interaction between a financial security system and its individual members. This model is employed in both rate making and the determination of reserves, two of the important functions that actuaries perform.

Introduction

In many scientific disciplines a simplified model of a complex reality has aided understanding. By clearing away much of the distracting and confusing detail, a model reduces a complicated reality to its essential elements. A well-conceived model becomes an important and useful tool in the study of complex systems.

There are many examples of physical models — e.g., the geographers' maps and the architects' construction models — but models may also be conceptual or mathematical. Mathematical models of financial security systems are the important tools of actuarial science.

Financial security systems can be modeled as if they consisted of two cash flows, one the flow into the system (the + or income flow), the other the flow of money out (the − or disbursement flow). For many systems, actuaries model the interactions of the system with an individual, the cash flows being those associated with an individual insurance policy, an individual annuity contract, or some other individual arrangement.

This chapter will put together random variables (Chapter III) and the time value of money (Chapter IV) to develop the general form of a model that actuaries have developed for the analysis of financial security systems of the individual type. Other actuarial models, for systems that are better represented on a collective or group basis, are the subject of Chapter VI.

A Generalized Individual Model

A cash flow *from* a financial security system is a time-related complex of payments. Every *disbursement* payment has the following elements: (1) a time t at which the payment is made, (2) an amount A_t , and (3) a probability of payment p_t . The amount A_t may be 0 or any other fixed amount, or it may be the expected value of a random variable. The probability p_t can have the value 0 or 1 (implying certainty as to whether the payment will be made), or it may lie somewhere between (implying uncertainty).

The cash flow *to* a financial security system is also a time-related payment complex. Every income payment has the same three elements, a time, an amount, and a probability. To avoid confusion between income and disbursement flows, t', $A_{t'}$, and $p_{t'}$, will replace the symbols t, A_t, and p_t whenever income payments are the focus.

The actuarial present value of a disbursement payment potentially payable t years hence is

$$(1+i)^{-t}p_tA_t,$$

where $(1+i)^{-t}$ is the discount for the time value of money at an assumed rate i, p_t is the probability that a payment will be made at time t, and A_t is the expected amount of such payment.

The actuarial present value of the entirety of potential future disbursements with respect to the individual is this same expression, summed over all positive values of t and can be written as

$$V_D = \Sigma(1+i)^{-t}p_tA_t,$$

Similarly, the actuarial present value of future income payments is

$$V_I = \Sigma(1+i)^{-t'} p_{t'} A_{t'},$$

where the summation is over all positive values of t' for which the product exists.

The essence of the Generalized Individual Model is the comparison of the actuarial present value of all future disbursement flows (V_D) with the actuarial present value of all future income flows (V_I), where both flows are those associated with an individual, and where the probabilities that the payments will be made, as well as the time value of money, are taken into account. The future, in this context, is measured from a time t_0, where this arbitrary zero point may vary from one application to another. The focus of the Generalized Individual Model is on the difference between V_D and V_I, which we here indicate by $\triangle$, defined by the equation

$$\triangle = V_D - V_I.$$

$\triangle$, however, clearly changes with time, and hence must be viewed as a function of "time since t_0," which we hereafter denote as k. The $\triangle$ at time k is defined by

$$\triangle(k) = V_D(k) - V_I(k),$$

and denotes what actuaries call the reserve at time k. The reserve, then, is the excess of the actuarial present value of future disbursements over the actuarial present value of future income.

In the normal course of events, the Generalized Individual Model is employed in two phases. In the first, the $\triangle(0)$, measured from the time when the individual arrangement begins, is set at 0, indicating an initial balance between the actuarial present values of disbursement and income flows. From this relationship the values of $A_{t'}$ (the considerations or premiums charged the individual) can be determined. Then in the second phase, $\triangle(k)$ defines the value of the reserve at any duration k.

Here, this model is expressed in very general form, but it can be specialized to represent almost any financial security system of the individual type. Two examples should suffice to illustrate the generality of the model.

Illustration 1—A Short-Term Insurance

There is a wide variety of financial security systems (most of which can also be considered insurance) where the contractual relationships with the individual are short-term. The period over which income is collected is short (often no longer than one year), and the period of potential disbursements is somewhat longer (because of the time required to adjudicate and pay claims). Property/casualty policies issued to individuals are perhaps the most notable examples, but there are short-term forms of individual life and health insurance as well.

As a first specialization of the generalized individual model for the short-term case, let
(1) Time be measured in years from the date of issue.
(2) The outgo be 0 for all values of t except $t=1$. There, A_t is the expected or mean value of the claim amount distribution; and the corresponding p_t is the probability of a claim occurring sometime in the period $t=0$ to $t=1$.
(3) The income at time 0 is π; elsewhere it is 0.
(4) $\triangle(0)$ is set equal to 0.

Then the solution of (4) above for π yields the pure claim cost, or the premium for a single year (without provision for expenses or security loading). [Note the assumption here that claims, on the average, are paid at the end of the policy year.

Some assumption as to claim payment timing is needed, but this particular assumption is not vital to the validity of the model.]

For a second specialization of the same model to the same short-term insurance, consider $\triangle(1)$ on the same policy, *after* a claim event has occurred but *before* any claim payment has been made. Then the expected value of future income becomes 0, and the expected value of future disbursements becomes

$$(1+i)^{-j}A_j.$$

Here j represents the present estimate of the time (measured from $t=1$) until this claim will be paid, and A_j represents the estimated amount thereof. The resulting

$$\triangle(1) = (1+i)^{-j}A_j$$

becomes the reserve (or liability) for claims incurred but unpaid. [Note that A_j is not necessarily equal to the A_t from the premium model, because enough information may be available to distinguish the amount of the specific claim from the overall average of the claim distribution.]

Illustration 2 — A Long-Term Insurance

For individual contracts with a longer time frame, the model is essentially the same, though with different specifications. Long term specializations of the Generalized Individual Model are used in individual life, disability, and health insurance and in individual retirement arrangements. The specialization for one plan of individual life insurance (20 pay whole life insurance), outlined below, is only one example.

(1) Time is measured from policy issue.
(2) A_t is equal to unity at $t = 1/2, 3/2, 5/2, \ldots$ and 0 elsewhere, while the corresponding p_t's are $_{t-1|}q_x$ from a mortality table.

(3) $A_{t'}$ is equal to π_x at $t' = 0, 1, 2, \ldots, 19$ and 0 elsewhere, while the corresponding $p_{t'}$'s are $_{t'}p_x$'s from the same mortality table.

(4) $\triangle(0)$ is 0.

These specializations make it possible to solve for π_x, the net level premium for \$1 of 20 pay whole life insurance, death claims payable in the middle of the policy year of death, for an insured age x at issue, all based on an assumed rate of interest and an assumed mortality table.

Having determined π_x, the actuary employs the same model, but with the future measured from k years after issue, to find

$$\triangle_k = V_D(k) - V_I(k) =$$
the net level premium reserve after k years.

For values of k greater than 20, the negative term drops out, all premiums due having been paid, and the reserve becomes simply the actuarial present value of future claim payments.

The Concept of Reserves

After the inception of an individual arrangement, and before its eventual termination, the reserves calculated via the generalized model are normally positive. Reserves are positive whenever the actuarial present value of the remaining disbursement flows exceeds the actuarial present value of the remaining income flows. Positive reserves are a natural consequence of income (premium) flows being earlier in time than disbursement (claim) flows.

While the model leads to the interpretation of reserves as a system liability, reserves have an asset interpretation as well. The system's liability is also the individual's asset (though the individual may have no right to convert the asset to cash). In another sense, the reserve is the measure of the assets expected to have arisen from the past operation of the individual arrangement.

Because the reserve, in all of its several interpretations, is fundamental to all branches of actuarial science, it must be included in any work on fundamental actuarial concepts.

More Sophisticated Applications of the Generalized Individual Model

The illustrations of this chapter present only a start toward the many applications of the generalized model. Expenses, as well as claim payments, can enter the disbursement side of the model, as can dividends, ancillary benefits, and provision for profit. The possibility that premiums will not be paid when due can enter the income side. Certain specializations will produce cash values, natural reserves, or modified premium reserves for long term insurance, or unearned premium reserves for short term. The model can also be arranged to produce the important reserve for incurred but unreported claims and the associated claim adjustment expenses. The model can be applied to the contract between a resident and a Continuing Care Community. Because of the wide reach of the generalized model to so many of the matters with which actuaries are concerned, the model itself becomes a fundamental concept.

Summary

The Generalized Individual Model can be specialized, in many ways not illustrated here, to give a good representation of the more complex features of financial retirement systems.

Some form of the long-term individual model is commonly used by actuaries working with individual life, disability, or health insurance, or individual annuities. Actuaries working with property/casualty insurance make more use of the short-term individual model.

The ability to manipulate the individual model, and to employ it effectively for a wide variety of financial security plans, is one of the distinguishing characteristics of the professional actuary. The model itself, and its natural consequence, the actuarial reserve, are among the fundamental concepts of actuarial science.

References

Bowers, Newton L., Jr., Hans U. Gerber, James C. Hickman, Donald A. Jones, and Cecil J. Nesbitt. *Actuarial Mathematics*. Itasca, Ill.: Society of Actuaries, 1986.

Foundations of Casualty Actuarial Science. New York: Casualty Actuarial Society, forthcoming.

Jewell, W.S. "Models in Insurance: Paradigms, Puzzles, Communications, and Revolutions." *Transactions of the 21st International Congress of Actuaries* S(1980): 87-141.

Jordan, Chester W., Jr. *Life Contingencies*. 2d ed. Chicago: Society of Actuaries, 1967.

Neill, Alistair. *Life Contingencies*. London: Heinemann, 1977.

O'Grady, Francis T. *Individual Health Insurance*. Itasca, Ill.: Society of Actuaries, 1988.

Chapter VI

Collective Models

Models appropriate for the analysis of employee benefit plans, social insurance, and other collective arrangements retain some of the characteristics of the individual model of Chapter V, but employ a different interpretation of "balance."

Introduction

The Generalized Individual Model of the previous chapter strikes a balance between the income and outgo flows associated with the interaction of a financial security system with an individual. Although the model is conceptually individual-by-individual, for many purposes the actuary must deal with aggregates — the sum of premiums, reserves, claims, and other items arising from a number of individual arrangements. Viewing a block of individual contracts as the sum of its individual parts is a practical procedure that does not require a new conceptual model, though for practical reasons some aggregating techniques may be required.

Several important financial security systems, however, have characteristics which require the use of a collective model. The balance between future income and future outgo is no longer on an individual-by-individual basis, but instead involves some sorting of these individual coverages into groups, and the striking of the balance group-by-group. In the extreme, the entire system may be aggregated.

This chapter makes no attempt to present a generalized collective model, because no such model seems to exist. Instead it presents three of the collective models that actuaries employ in the analysis of employee benefit plans and social insurance.

Employee Benefit Plans

Employee benefit plans are financial security systems sponsored by employers, by unions, or both, under which some part of the worker's remuneration is in the form of benefits other than cash. One of the earliest is the workers' compensation plan, developed early in the twentieth century under the impetus of emerging state law regarding an employer's responsibility for the financial consequence of work-related injury or illness. Other types of employee benefit plans developing later are group life, disability and health arrangements, and employee retirement plans.

All but the last of these, retirement or pension plans, tend to be relatively short term in nature, in so far as the contractual arrangements are concerned.

We find that we can fit most of these short term employee benefit plans into what we will here call the group model.

Group Model

The group model, as the term is used here, is applicable to workers' compensation and most forms of group insurance. The model is also appropriate for employee benefits of a self-administered nature, where the involvement of an insurance company, if any, is limited to the provision of administrative services.

Because the group model applies to contractual arrangements that are short-term in nature, it is not greatly different from the short-term individual model. However, in the modeling of both premiums and reserves, the group model tends to be less structured and less precise. The rate charged for any one employee is unimportant, as only the aggregate rate is needed. The group to which the model is applied is necessarily a continuously changing collection of covered individuals. It is essentially the aggregated character and the dynamic quality of the group model that distinguishes it from the more precise and more static individual short-term model.

In the setting of an initial premium rate, the emphasis is on the pure insurance cost for a unit of coverage, where the unit is the employee, the face amount of the insurance, or the payroll. To the extent that classification variables (such as age, sex, occupation, dependents, etc.) within the covered group are taken into account, pure insurance costs are the weighted averages of the assumed rate and amount of claims for each of the classifications. Appropriate provisions for expenses, risk and profit are then added to these pure insurance costs. Finally, there may be some adjustment for what is known about the actual experience of the same case in the recent past, and/or for the competitive situation. The premium rate eventually developed may be paid in part by the employee through payroll deduction, but the remainder is paid by the employer.

For the relatively short period during which the initial rates are guaranteed, the premium changes only as the number of coverage units change, as some employees drop out and others are added. In renewal years, there is often a renegotiation of the unit rate. The employer may wish to change the benefit package; but even if benefits stay steady, claim costs in general may have risen (especially true of group medical plans), or the actual experience for the case in question may have been better or worse than anticipated. The methods devised for returning some part of the past surplus, or for making up past deficits, as a part of the renewal or renegotiation process, become an important part of the practical model. A term often used in connection with these methods is "experience rating."

The important reserves arising from the group model are those for claims incurred but not yet paid (including those not yet reported), and for premiums paid but not yet earned. These are similar, in concept, to the reserves produced by the short-term individual model.

Defined Benefit Pension Plan Model

A form of employee benefit plan which clearly does not fit the group model is the retirement or pension plan. Here the income to the system occurs at a much earlier point of time than the payment of retirement benefits, so the time value of money plays a most important role.

Retirement plans of two quite different forms have evolved. One of these, the defined contribution form, has the characteristics of the individual savings plan or the individual deferred annuity. For actuarial purposes another specialization of the Generalized Individual Model, with reserves calculated retrospectively, is the most appropriate. No collective model is needed.

The model for defined benefit retirement plans, however, has the long-term characteristics of the long-term individual model, but the collective characteristics of the employee benefit plan. The defined benefit model becomes the second of the three collective models described in this chapter.

The actuarial cost methods that have evolved for use with defined benefit pension plans have been classified into two relatively distinct groups. The model for the first of these groups has much in common with the Generalized Individual Model described earlier, because the contribution required for the group is essentially the sum of the contributions calculated for each covered individual. The actuarial cost methods once known as unit credit, entry age normal, and individual level premium are of this "individual" type. Though collective techniques may be needed in the amortization of the initial accrued liability or in the adjustments for actuarial gain or loss, the model commonly employed is basically the individual model. The "accrued liability" plays much the same role as the "reserve" under long-term individual arrangements.

The second general class of actuarial cost methods for defined benefit retirement plans has different characteristics. Under the various forms of the "aggregate" actuarial cost method, the balance between the present value of future outgo and the present value of future income only applies for the sum of all currently covered individuals, and does not apply individually.

The actuarial assumptions needed in the typical defined benefit pension calculation are not only those with respect to mortality, retirement, disability, and withdrawal of employees, but also economic variables such as rates of salary/wage increase, and in some plans rates of price inflation. The rate of investment return, and particularly the interaction of this rate with rates of wage and price inflation, plays a very important role.

As in the group model, the benefits taken into account in a typical defined benefit pension calculation are only those for active employees (and former employees with remaining benefits). The group to whom the model is being applied is dynamic, continually changing as some individuals leave the group and others join. Typically the model of a continually changing closed group is sufficient. When it is, no assumptions need be made regarding employees to be hired in the future.

Actuaries have, however, made some use of an open group model for defined benefit pension plans. Such a model requires an assumption about the number and the characteristics of those to be employed in the future. The open group model provides further insight, especially if the actuarial cost method chosen is one of the aggregate types. The theoretical development of open group models dates back to the mid-twentieth century, and the open group approach to actual pension funding is now of some practical use.

The defined benefit pension model is capable of extension to other types of benefits. One example is post-retirement employee benefits other than pensions, such as life and health benefits. Although the pre-retirement funding of such benefits continues to present practical difficulties, corporate accounting on a pre-retirement charging basis is of developing concern. Another related area of burgeoning interest is the financing of continuing care retirement communities. These are fields in which actuarial expertise will, of necessity, be increasingly engaged.

The Social Insurance Model

The model for the U.S. Social Security System, and for other social insurance, differs from the models previously discussed in that the model must be open rather than closed. The balance struck is between the projection of disbursements over a very long time period and the projection of income over the same period, not only with respect to present participants, but with respect to their successors as well.

Actuaries working with social insurance must become students of demography, and use demographical techniques to project the covered population. Among the assumptions needed for the demographic aspect of the projections are mortality rates, disability rates, fertility rates, marriage and divorce rates, and rates of immigration less emigration.

Because benefits are wage related and adjusted for inflation, economic assumptions are also required. Among these are rates of wage inflation, price inflation, medical expense inflation, and unemployment. Assumptions are also necessary for the choices that individuals make, especially regarding the time they apply for retirement benefits, and the extent to which they may work thereafter.

In many ways, the social insurance model is as sophisticated as any employed by actuaries. It is the best example available of a collective and open-ended model of a very complicated financial security system serving a huge population.

Summary

The Generalized Individual Model is sometimes useful in the modeling of the interactions of financial security systems with groups of individuals. This will be the case if the collective arrangement can be logically viewed as an aggregate of individual arrangements.

The group model presented here has much in common with the Generalized Individual Model applied to short-term arrangements, though the model is necessarily less precise, and involves collective principles.

The defined benefit pension model has something in common with the Generalized Individual Model applied to long-term arrangements, though it sometimes requires techniques outside the individual approach, and may take on open-group characteristics.

The social insurance model uses no individual techniques, is entirely open-ended, and takes many of the characteristics of future demographic and economic projections.

References

Group Model
Michelbacher, G. F. "The Practice of Experience Rating." *Proceedings of the Casualty Actuarial Society* 4(1917-18): 293-324.

Whitney, Albert W. "The Theory of Experience Rating." *Proceedings of the Casualty Actuarial Society* 4(1917-18): 274-292.

Pension and Retirement Model
Actuarial Standards Board. Retiree Health Care Committee. *Actuarial Standard of Practice Measuring and Allocating Actuarial Present Values of Retiree Health Care and Death Benefits.* Washington DC: Actuarial Standards Board, 1988.

American Academy of Actuaries. *An Actuary's Guide to Compliance with Statement of Financial Accounting Standards No. 87.* Washington, DC: American Academy of Actuaries, 1986.

Anderson, Arthur W. *Pension Mathematics for Actuaries.* Needham, Mass.: Arthur W. Anderson, 1985.

Bowers, Newton L., Jr., James C. Hickman, and Cecil J. Nesbitt. "The Dynamics of Pension Funding: Contribution Theory." *Transactions of the Society of Actuaries* 31(1979): 93-136.

Doran, Phyllis A., Kenneth D. MacBain, and William A. Reimert. *Measuring and Funding Corporate Liabilities for Retiree Health Benefits.* Washington: Employee Benefit Research Institute, 1987.

Interim Actuarial Standards Board. Pension Committee. *Recommendations for Actuarial Communications Related to Statements of Financial Accounting Standards Nos. 87 and 88.* Washington, DC: American Academy of Actuaries, 1987.

Interim Actuarial Standards Board. Pension Committee. *Recommendations for Measuring Pension Obligations.* Washington, DC: American Academy of Actuaries, 1988.

Interim Actuarial Standards Board. Specialty Committee. Committee on Continuing Care Retirement Communities. *Actuarial Standards of Practice Relating to Continuing Care Retirement Communities.* Washington, DC: American Academy of Actuaries, 1987.

Schnitzer, Robert J. "Characteristics and Operation of Projection Valuation Methods for Pension Plan Funding." *Transactions of the Society of Actuaries* 29(1977): 269-314.

Trowbridge, C. L. "Fundamentals of Pension Funding." *Transactions of the Society of Actuaries* 4(1952): 17-43.

Social Insurance Model

Andrews, George H. and John A. Beekman. *Actuarial Projections for the Old-Age, Survivors, and Disability Insurance Program of Social Security in the United States of America*. Itasca, Ill.: Actuarial Education and Research Fund, 1987.

Keyfitz, Nathan. *Introduction to the Mathematics of Population*. Rev. ed., Reading, Mass.: Addison-Wesley, 1977.

Chapter VII

Classification, Selection and Antiselection

The cluster of ideas surrounding classification, selection, and antiselection are fundamental actuarial concepts. The statistical element is the sorting of risks into homogenous classifications, and the estimation of the appropriate probability for each; but the psychological component is of at least equal importance. Human beings can be expected to act on their perception of their own best interests, and to select against any system that permits choices.

Introduction

For many different purposes and in many different forms, modern society has found it necessary to establish groupings or classifications. We classify the labor force by age, sex, and occupation, count the population by place of residence, and recognize differences by religion, national origin, and socio-economic class. We educate children using a classification system based largely on chronological age, though we may also separate the handicapped, the slow learners, or the gifted from the main body through the concept of "special education." In criminal law, we distinguish felonies from misdemeanors, and classify within each—all for the purpose of a rational system of justice.

To the extent that these classifications affect the treatment of people, questions of discrimination or fairness may arise. We find attitudes about these matters that run the entire range from egalitarianism, the identical treatment of all, to the sharply contrasting philosophy that individuals should be treated in accordance with their specific characteristics.

This chapter concerns itself with classification within financial security systems, and hence those forms of classification of most concern to the actuary. The categories or classes into which individuals are to be sorted, usually but not always for pricing purposes, constitute the classification system. The process by which a financial security system determines the category appropriate for each individual is here viewed as selection. The tendency for individuals to exploit, or select against, classification and selection will be called antiselection. A constant interplay between selective and antiselective forces is inherent in financial security systems.

Homogeneity of Risk

The importance of the concept of homogeneity, as it applies to classification within a financial security system, is demonstrated by means of the following hypothetical situation:

Assume that an insurance benefit of A is to be paid upon the occurrence of a designated random event; and that the price (premium) is based on the assumption that the probability of this event occurring is q. The value q has been estimated by observing the number of events and non-events in large samples of the potential population.

Assume further that the population is truly risk-averse with respect to the insured against event, and that *for every individual q* is a good estimate of the probability. Under these conditions it seems likely that buyers will be found, and hence that the insurance offering will be successful, even though the price must be considerably more than the value of expected claims, Aq.

But now abandon the last of the above assumptions, and assume instead that probabilities for two (or more) sub-groups within the population may be *unequal* . It follows that the proportion q is not a true probability based on homogenous data, but is instead a mix of two (or more) sub-group probabilities. For some sub-groups, the probability is greater than q, for others less than q. Is it now appropriate to base the pricing for all subgroups on q? Or is it now necessary to vary the probability assumption, and hence the price, by sub-group?

To examine this important question, make the simplifying assumption that there are only sub-groups (classifications) a and b, and that in the samples from which the estimate of q was derived classes a and b are of equal size. Let the true probability for class a be $q+\triangle$; then that for class b must be $q-\triangle$. Assume further that this kind of insurance is truly voluntary, and that $\triangle$ is of sufficient size that cost differences are meaningful. We now examine the question of how many of the potential buyers from classes a and b will actually buy, if the rate charged is based on q.

It seems almost certain the higher risk class a will readily buy at the "bargain" rate based on q, while the lower risk sub-group b, facing an "overcharge" in q, will not. The proportion k of actual buyers (as opposed to potential buyers) from class a will then exceed 1/2, while the proportion of actual buyers from class b will be less than 1/2. Antiselection has occurred, and the premium charged, based on q, has become inadequate. This follows from the relationship

$$k(q+\triangle) + (1-k)(q-\triangle) > q \text{ where } k > 0.5 \text{ and } \triangle > 0$$

Antiselection may be avoided if the buying public is unaware that the difference $\triangle$ exists. Antiselection may be overcome if a strongly risk averse population has no viable alternative. But neither of these circumstances can be expected to last in a competitive market. As information becomes more widespread, and as competing insurance carriers strive to attract the better risks, the less refined classification system must ultimately give way to the more refined.

Evolution of a Classification System — Individual Life Insurance

The early history of individual life insurance may be a good starting point for the study of how and why classification systems have evolved. The early forms of what we now call life insurance may be in the nearly-forgotten past, but one of the earliest was assessment insurance.

The assessment concept was very simple. A group of people agreed that a unit of death benefit would be paid to the beneficiary of any member of the group who might die within the next year; and that the money would come from equal assessments against members still alive at the end of the year. While there may have been some health requirements for an applicant to join the group (and in that sense a rudimentary "in or out" classification system was employed), assessments were independent of age. For pricing purposes, attained age was not a classification variable. Antiselection should have been expected, and not surprisingly, it occurred.

The assessment principle enjoyed a period of prosperity, based partly on the simplicity of the basic concept. Eventually, however, once the public recognized that mortality rates increase with age, sales at the younger ages became increasingly difficult and younger members were dropping out, while older prospects or members exhibited the opposite tendencies. The average age of the covered group rose, as did the assessment calls. Non-recognition of age as a pricing factor was clearly at the root of these troubles, and had to be abandoned. Even the most successful of the assessment companies found it necessary to adopt attained age as a major classification variable, and age is still the primary classification variable in life insurance as it exists today.

The first half of the twentieth century saw refinement in individual life insurance selection or classification procedures. Aside from the primary classification (age), applicants were classified only by "standard versus substandard," but, within the latter, by varying degrees of "impairment." To make these distinctions, life com panies relied on information obtained from questions asked on the application, from physical examinations, height, weight, and blood-pressure measurements, attending physicians' statements, and reports of inspection agencies. A high percent of all applicants were thrown into the very broad "standard" class with the lowest premium rates, while the remainder, considered "substandard" for reasons of health, occupation, or behavior, were either declined or offered insurance at higher premium rates. The proper classification of insurance risks, particularly those viewed as substandard, became a special "underwriting" skill that life insurance companies had to develop.

Mortality tables published by the U.S. Government from census data have long shown that males experience higher mortality rates than females, and that the differences are both substantial and growing. Despite this and other evidence of female mortality superiority, the life insurance industry was slow to adopt gender as a classification variable. For quite some time the rationale for female life insurance rates no lower than those for males lay in compensating factors in the expense area; though the real reason may have been that females bought very little insurance, and the change might not have been worth the trouble. The first use of sex-distinct mortality tables for pricing purposes came in annuities and life income settlement options, where female risks predominate. Eventually gender distinctions became common in life insurance pricing as well.

A more recent development, and a rather dramatic one, is the recognition of smoking as a classification factor. Evidence that smoking shortens life expectancy had been accumulating even before the U.S. Surgeon General dramatized this issue in a 1964 report. Life insurance companies started to accumulate the information necessary to study smoker/non-smoker mortality in an insurance setting, and by now a large part of the industry uses smoking as a classification factor.

More Complex Classification – Property and Casualty Insurance

The sorting out of life insurance applicants in accordance with a best estimate of the probability of death is by no means a simple matter; but establishment of a classification system is more complicated for casualty actuaries. Here the problem is not only the likelihood of a claim, but also the amount of the claim if one occurs. There are also problems of identifying the basic unit for which a rate applies, and of a multiplicity of coverages wrapped up in a single policy contract.

As an example of these complications, take the typical automobile insurance policy. The intent is to offer coverage for most of the perils associated with owning an automobile, so the total coverage has features of property, health, accident, and liability insurance. Although the basic unit is a specific automobile, rates will vary with the liability limits, deductibles, and other details of the coverage.

Among the several classification variables commonly employed today are these:
  (a) the geographical location where the automobile is based
  (b) the type, make, and age of the automobile
  (c) how a vehicle is used, and the distance it is driven
  (d) the age, sex, training, and driving records of the principal drivers.

Once classifications have been established, statistics can be gathered for the purpose of determining a rate (or rating factor) for each cell in the complex matrix. It is usually necessary that the data gathering be on an industry-wide (or nearly so) basis, since no one insurer will have enough exposure for all of the many combinations.

The choice of the variables to be recognized in the classification system is all important, as is the degree of refinement attempted. The primary goal – homogeneity of the frequencies within each cell—can be accomplished only approximately, and there are other considerations as well. The information needed to assign each automobile its correct rate must be reasonably obtainable. At least as important, the classification system must be defensible, both to the regulators and to the general public.

Classification and Selection in Employee Benefit Plans

The classification and selection issues treated to this point have this in common: the purchase decision is largely up to the individual, as to whether to buy at all, whom to buy from, and in what amount. In contrast, the employee benefit plan gives the individual very little choice in these matters, and thus has very different classification and selection characteristics. For purposes of illustration here, we use the typical employee medical/dental plan offered by health insurers, Blue Cross and Blue Shield organizations (the Blues), and HMOs.

The crucial difference between employee benefit plans and individual insurance lies in the employer's role as payor of much (if not all) of the cost. As sponsor and largest contributor, the employer is often the determiner of plan design. Although the employees and their dependents are seldom required to join an employee health plan, they are easily induced to do so by the presence of the employer's substantial contribution, a form of non-cash compensation that the non-joining employee forfeits.

From the insurer's point of view, the purpose of classification is the determination of an appropriate price for the group, not for each individual insured. Safeguards against individual antiselection are of relatively little importance, and are often limited to the requirement that the worker be actively employed when the insurance becomes effective, and joins when first eligible.

Antiselection by individuals remains a factor, however, even in employee benefit plans. Employees have some area of choice in most such plans, and considerable choice in some. The option to include dependents is one possibility. The "cafeteria" type, where employees select among several different benefit packages, gives the worker the opportunity to meet particular needs, but it also leads to antiselection. An HMO option, or a conversion privilege, are other examples. In employee benefit plans, however, the antiselection affects the employer's compensation system more than it does the insurer. That the high risk employee enjoys more valuable insurance than his low risk associate, yet contributes no more, is simply a part of employee benefit plan philosophy.

Despite the relative unimportance of individual antiselection, however, classification systems for pricing purposes play an important role. It has been characteristic of the insurance companies in the group health field to take into account, for pricing purposes, such classification variables as age, sex, location and income distributions, the industry, and the claim experience of the same group in the past.

The Blues and HMOs, on the other hand, have tended, at least initially, to follow "community rating" principles, where the rates for groups are independent of the characteristics of the group. Because groups as well as individuals are price conscious and tend to buy where they can find the lowest rate, the more refined system attracts the lower risk groups, leaving the higher risk groups to the community rating organizations. As we saw in individual insurance, the more refined classification system eventually supersedes the less refined, unless financial security systems using the latter have other competitive advantages.

Public Acceptance

Classification systems used by insurance organizations have always been considered a matter in which the public has a legitimate interest. Government has given insurance regulators the responsibility to see that insurance pricing is adequate but not exorbitant, and that it is not unfairly discriminatory. Because the principle of homogeneity of risk is sometimes in direct conflict with public perceptions of fairness or justice, classification systems used by insurance organizations have been under considerable attack in recent years.

Part of the reason is that the civil rights movement has effectively outlawed discrimination in many areas, especially that based on race, sex, national origin, religion—and sometimes age, sexual preference, or handicaps. The distinction between unfair discrimination and any discrimination is unclear at best, so the classification of insurance risks by such variables as age or sex becomes suspect, and may require elaborate justification. On the other hand, the ignoring of any significant underwriting variable, on the grounds of public acceptance, leads to dangers of subsidization, when demonstrably poor risks are pooled with the good.

Problems with public acceptance are especially difficult when the insurance is only semi-voluntary in nature, and when there may be an apparent discrimination against one of the protected groups. An automobile owner or a home buyer finds that insurance is almost mandatory, so an applicant who finds himself in an unfavorable pricing classification, for reasons over which he has little or no control, may consider himself a victim of the system. Inner-city dwellers, charged more for automobile or homeowners insurance because of high levels of theft or vandalism, have, in their opinion, a just complaint.

Antiselection—More Generally

The important principle that human beings will tend to act in their own financial interest, and in so doing may select against the system as a whole, is an extension of the utility theory of Chapter II. It is much more general than the question of who can obtain insurance and at what rate. By their very nature, financial security systems offer choices, meeting the individual's need for flexibility, and making the system more attractive. Where choices can be permitted without undue damage to others within the system, or to the system as a whole, they are likely to be incorporated.

Examples of commonly offered choices are the non-forfeiture and dividend options of individual life insurance, the choice of annuity forms in retirement plans, the choice of coverages under "cafeteria" plans, and the choice of the age at which a Social Security benefit begins. These choices are permitted on the basis of actuarial equivalence, under which all choices are said to have the same actuarial present value—but this equivalence depends upon a specified set of actuarial assumptions, which seldom hold for an individual case. Some adverse selection is inevitable, but with adequate safeguards it can often be controlled.

There are other situations where antiselection is expected, or even intended. Conversion privileges under group insurance policies are an example. The privilege is thought to be in the public interest, is required by insurance law, and is paid for (generally) by the employer.

Summary

The cluster of ideas surrounding classification, selection, and antiselection is a fundamental actuarial concept. The statistical element is the sorting of risks into homogenous classifications, and the estimation of the appropriate probability for each; but the psychological component is at least equally important. Human beings can be expected to act on their perception of their own best interests, and to select against any system that permits choices. They can also be expected to protest when limitations on choice are proposed, or when classification systems conflict with other criteria of human rights.

References

Cummins, J. David, Barry D. Smith, R. Neil Vance, and Jack L. Van Derhei. *Risk Classification in Life Insurance*. Boston: Kluwer-Nijhoff, 1983.

Gore, John K. "Should Life Companies Discriminate against Women?" *Transactions of the Actuarial Society of America* 6(1899–1900): 380-388.

Hunter, Arthur. "Mortality among Women." *Transactions of the Actuarial Society of America* 11(1909–1910): 446-450.

Lew, Edward A. and Lawrence Garfinkel. "Differences in Mortality and Longevity by Sex, Smoking Habits, and Health Status." *Transactions of the Society of Actuaries* 39(1987): 107-130.

MacIntyre, Duncan M. *Health Insurance and Rate Making*. Ithaca, N.Y.: Cornell University Press, 1962.

Promislow, S. David. "Measurement of Equity." *Transactions of the Society of Actuaries* 39(1987): 215-256.

Society of Actuaries. "Report of the General Committee on Publication of Monetary Tables, Section II. Female Extension of the 1958 CSO and CET Mortality Tables." *Transactions of the Society of Actuaries* 11(1959): 1060-1069.

Stone, James M. "Excerpt from the Opinion, Findings, and Decision on 1978 Automobile Insurance Rates." Part II of *Automobile Insurance Risk Classification: Equity and Accuracy*. Boston: Division of Insurance, Commonwealth of Massachusetts, 1978.

Woll, Richard G. "A Study of Risk Assessment." *Proceedings of the Casualty Actuarial Society* 66(1979): 84-138.

Chapter VIII

Assumptions, Conservatism and Adjustment

Actuarial calculations are necessarily based on assumptions regarding the future. Important practical considerations influence the actuary in his decisions relating to the level of conservatism to be reflected in those assumptions. In the long run, actual experience replaces assumptions, through the mechanism of an adjustment system.

Introduction

A high percentage of all actuarial calculations is based on one or more actuarial assumptions. A calculation is often the answer to a "what, if" question. What is the present value of $1 per annum payable in perpetuity, if the rate of interest (i) is a constant 4%? In this very simple example, the answer, $1/0.04 = 25$, is valid only if i is 0.04.

The assumption, although it may be based on experience of the past, is ordinarily about the uncertain future. The answer obtained is no better than the assumption behind it.

In the early stages of training, the actuary learns to make calculations of this "what, if" type. Although the problems can be much more difficult than the simple example cited (usually because there is more than one assumption, and a higher degree of mathematical complexity is involved), actuarial mathematics is the only tool needed; provided that any assumptions are treated as given. Using the same assumptions, two actuaries should arrive at very similar, if not identical, answers.

Much more difficult, and certainly more important, is the determination of appropriate assumptions. In the real world the assumptions are *not* given, and actuaries have to choose their own. It is easily shown that the results obtained from most actuarial calculations are sensitive to the assumptions employed; and hence that the answers reached depend upon the assumptions chosen.

This chapter is devoted to questions such as these. What are conservative as opposed to unconservative assumptions? Are actuarial assumptions predictions? Are they estimates? What are the consequences when an assumption proves to be very wrong? What are the best methods of dealing with these consequences?

Conservatism

By actuarial conservatism we mean the use of any actuarial technique (usually but not always the choice of one or more assumptions) that leads to a higher price for a set of benefits, or a higher value of a liability. Clearly, conservatism is a relative term, operating over a continuum. The question is less often one of "whether," more often one of "how much."

Present values are generally inversely a function of the discount rate; thus the assumption of a low discount rate adds to the price or to the liability, and is hence more conservative. The assumption of a higher rate of discount is usually less conservative.

In health, property, or casualty insurance, use of a high estimate for frequency or severity is conservative. In life insurance, an assumption of a higher rate of mortality adds to the price or the liability, and is thus conservative; but the reverse is true if a life annuity benefit is the focus of attention. For disability benefits, high rates of disability incidence and low rates of disability termination are conservative. For defined benefit pension plans, low assumptions as to employee death or withdrawal rates, and low rates of interest are conservative; but low rates of assumed salary increase are less conservative.

In general, if a benefit is contingent upon the happening of a random event, an assumption that the probability of that happening is high will be more conservative, that the probability is lower will be less conservative. Should the benefit be contingent on the non-happening of the same event, the foregoing statement must be reversed.

No value judgments are to be implied from the above definition. Whether actuarial conservatism is good or bad is not at issue at this point. A discussion of conservatism from the actuarial viewpoint will be deferred until later in this chapter.

The Uncertain Future

Actuarial assumptions often, though not invariably, relate to a long span of time, not infrequently fifty or more years. The ability of humans to predict even short-range future events is severely limited, and forecasting ability diminishes rapidly as the time span lengthens. Predictions are often based on "extrapolation" or "the continuance of present trends," but neither can be expected to hold up for very long. The actuary is particularly aware that he has no crystal ball, and that any prediction that he might venture will invariably prove to be wrong, in one direction or the other. He can be expected to resist the idea that the assumptions he uses are predictions, though the public often understands them as such.

If an actuarial assumption is not a prediction, then it may be better described as an estimate. Is it then the actuary's "best estimate" (presumably based on his interpretation of all the pertinent data that he can find)? A best estimate implies that the estimator picks the mean, median, or mode of his personal probability distribution. This view of an actuarial assumption may suit some actuaries, but others will find it deficient.

The Level of Conservatism

In certain situations, it is appropriate that actuaries will tend to be conservative (in the sense defined earlier). The reasons lie in the nature of the financial security systems with which actuaries are associated. Stated very generally, these reasons are (1) the actuary sees the public's interest as being better served by a conservative approach, and (2) the actuary sees the consequences of error on the conservative side as distinctly preferable to error in the opposite direction.

Conservative assumptions on the liability side of the balance sheet of an insurance enterprise are so generally considered to be in the public interest that state insurance regulation will usually require some conservatism. Conservatism in the determination of liabilities is an important part of the assurance of solvency. The principle that liabilities must be conservatively valued, and that assets must exceed liabilities, is inherent in insurance regulation, just as it is in the regulation of banks and other financial institutions that deal with the general public. There may be some question about how much conservatism is appropriate, but there is little disagreement that some conservatism is desirable, if not actually required, in the financial reports of most financial institutions.

In pricing, similar considerations are encountered. A system's solvency depends not only on the adequacy of its stated liabilities, but also on the adequacy of the prices that it charges. It is not in the public interest for a financial security system, whatever its nature, to become insolvent.

A related rationale for actuarial conservatism is found in the actuary's perception of the consequences of error. If costs are initially over-estimated (via the use of assumptions that later prove to have been too pessimistic), the emergence of actual experience is good news for someone. The beneficiary of this good result may be the insurance carrier, or it may be the customer who participates in this good experience. It may be the employer in a defined benefit pension plan, or the individual members of an association-type group health arrangement. Contrast these results with those that arise if the early estimates of plan costs were insufficient, and some or all of the affected parties find themselves confronted with the problem of how to deal with the "deficit."

Acting against the use of assumptions reflecting a high degree of conservatism is the question of equity. It may well be that the good effects of favorable experience flow to persons different from those who bore the initially higher costs. Equity or fairness between different classes of people is an important consideration in many of the financial security systems with which an actuary works.

To the extent that there is any inherent bias toward conservatism, that natural conservatism must be tempered by the realities of the environment in which the actuary finds himself. There are times for conservatism, others when conservatism is not appropriate.

Experience Adjustments

Because most of the financial security systems with which the actuary is associated are intended to last, and hence are in essence long term, and because true cost can only be determined as actual experience develops, a very important part of actuarial technique is an adjustment mechanism through which estimated costs are replaced, albeit slowly, by costs reflecting the actual experience.

A first example of a common adjustment mechanism is "participating" insurance. The assumptions which go into the initial pricing are deliberately conservative, so the early premiums are higher than they need be. Actuarial gains are expected; and as these develop, gains are returned to the insurance buyer in the form of "dividends."

The typical group arrangement uses a slightly different technique. Here the initial premium rate is guaranteed for only a short time, and rate changes occur frequently. The contract permits the insurer to change rates even if the benefit package remains unchanged, and the customer often chooses to change the benefits as well. For both of these reasons, and because the "mix" of employees is seldom static, rate renegotiations are very common. In the process, the rates charged and the developing experience can be brought into closer harmony; and this is frequently the result. The process is often called experience rating, and may be either prospective or retrospective. Credibility theory, first discussed in Chapter III, is an important tool.

There are several techniques used by pension actuaries to bring the actuarial assumptions and the actual plan experience together. These methods are commonly known as "actuarial gain/loss adjustment." Adjustment for emerging experience is typically an increase or decrease in the rate of future contribution. Such adjustment can be rapid or slow, or its pace may depend upon whether gain or loss is being experienced. There are government requirements in this area, just as there are in other phases of the pension actuary's work.

As a final example of how actuaries adjust for experience not in accordance with the initial assumptions, note how this is handled in U.S. Social Security. For quite some time, the actuaries employed by the Social Security Administration have published long-term projections based on multiple sets of actuarial assumptions. Currently there are four different sets. The two extremes are known as "optimistic" and "pessimistic." There are also two intermediate sets, one slightly more conservative than the other. All of these assumptions are updated annually.

Congress receives these projections, together with any recommendations that the executive branch of government chooses to make. The political process uses these projections, together with other considerations, to make occasional adjustments in benefits, tax rates, or both. Here the adjustment process is political rather than actuarial, but it is nonetheless an effective means for drawing estimate and actual experience together.

Under any of the above adjustment techniques, if the early estimates later prove to have been conservative, "actuarial gains" develop. These gains can then be used to reduce future outlays for the same benefit package, or can be employed to reduce the additional cost of benefit increases. On the other hand, actuarial losses, arising from over-optimism in the initial assumptions, lead to increases in future outlays or benefit cut-backs. The difficulty inherent when actuarial losses must somehow be made up, especially when compared with the ease of returning actuarial gains, is the reason previously noted why actuaries strongly prefer that their initial estimates have at least some degree of conservatism.

Another Manifestation of Conservatism

Although a certain amount of conservatism may be introduced through the choice of actuarial assumptions, there is another and more direct approach to the need for conservatism in a financial security system balance sheet. Although financial security systems are designed to reduce the economic risks of the individuals they serve, they do so by assuming risk themselves. Actuaries in North America are currently giving much thought to the setting up of explicit "contingency reserves," and relying less heavily on conservatism within the actuarial assumptions, to protect against the major economic risks that financial security systems run.

A Committee of the Society of Actuaries has identified three kinds of insurer risk for which specific statutory contingency reserves may be needed. The first, $C(1)$, is the risk of asset loss, the possibility that bonds or mortgages may go into default or that the stock market may decline. $C(2)$ refers to the risk of pricing insufficiency. Reinsurance may be relied upon as a partial hedge against adverse statistical fluctuation, but there are several other forms of pricing insufficiency that may in fact be more important. The risk of loss due to interest rate swings coupled with asset-liability mismatching is designated $C(3)$. Determination of an optimum size for each of these three contingency reserves, and especially for their total, is a challenging project in which many actuaries are engaged. This endeavor serves well as an example of actuarial conservatism in action.

Summary

Except where prohibited by law, or effectively barred by competition, actuaries tend to incorporate some degree of conservatism into their calculations and their recommendations. Often this is achieved through the use of actuarial assumptions thought to err on the conservative side, though the introduction of an explicit allowance for conservatism is another way of accomplishing the same objective.

The actuary's bias in favor of the conservative approach is based on a conception of the public interest, and on a preference for the results of erring on the conservative side as opposed to the consequences of the opposite kind of error.

For the systems with which they are associated, actuaries have worked out techniques for adjusting to actual experience. When these techniques work well, deviations of experience from what was initially assumed are taken care of in orderly fashion.

References

Individual Life Insurance Dividend Theory
Jackson, Robert T. "Some Observations on Ordinary Dividends." *Transactions of the Society of Actuaries* 11(1959): 764-811.

Maclean, Joseph B. and Edward W. Marshall. *Distribution of Surplus*. New York: Actuarial Society of America, 1937.

Group Insurance Experience Rating
Bolnick, Howard J. "Experience-Rating Group Life Insurance." *Transactions of the Society of Actuaries* 26(1975): 123-224.

Jackson, Paul H. "An Experience Rating Formula." *Transactions of the Society of Actuaries* 5(1953): 239-267.

Keffer, Ralph. "An Experience Rating Formula." *Transactions of Actuarial Society of America* 30(1929): 130-139.

Actuarial Gain/Loss Adjustment in Defined Benefit Plans

Anderson, Arthur W. *Pension Mathematics for Actuaries*. Needham, Mass.: Arthur W. Anderson, 1985.

U.S. Social Security

Andrews, George H. and John A. Beekman. *Actuarial Projections for the Old-Age, Survivors, and Disability Insurance Program of Social Security in the United States of America*. Itasca, Ill.: Actuarial Education and Research Fund, 1987.

Contingency Reserves

"Discussion of the Preliminary Report of the Committee on Valuation and Related Problems." *Record of the Society of Actuaries* 5, No. 1(1982): 241-284.

Milgrom, Paul R. "Measuring the Interest Rate Risk." *Transactions of the Society of Actuaries* 37(1985): 241-302.

Chapter IX

The Role of Fundamental Concepts in the Development of Standards

Introduction

This chapter gives further consideration to the role that fundamental concepts play in the development of actuarial standards. It then considers the practical problems that arise when two fundamental actuarial concepts appear to be in conflict, or when a fundamental actuarial concept is incongruent with law or strongly held public opinion.

Fundamental Concepts as a Step toward Standards

As stated in the opening paragraphs of Chapter I, this monograph is written under the assumption that actuarial standards must be based on fundamental actuarial concepts. Using building construction as an analogy, we think of the structure of standards as resting on the foundation of fundamental concepts, and hence use the term foundations as synonymous with fundamentals. Actuarial principles, as suggested in Chapter I, lie between standards and foundations. Principles might be likened to the walls and floors of the building, which rest on the foundations, but support the more specialized portions of the structure.

This monograph cannot anticipate the actuarial standards or actuarial principles that may eventually develop, but it may be useful to illustrate some of the ways in which foundations, principles, and standards might be interrelated.

Any standard with respect to the collection or the interpretation of data would necessarily be based on probability and statistics, the subject of Chapter III.

A standard on when discounting for interest is required, is optional, or is forbidden, and at what rates of interest, would be an extension of Chapter IV.

The Casualty Actuarial Society has already put forth a set of principles on property and casualty loss and loss adjustment expense reserves, and another set on property and casualty rate making. Both of these sets of principles are specializations of the fundamental concepts of Chapter V, and both may become the basis for standards.

The accounting profession has adopted a special form of the defined benefit pension model described in Chapter VI as a financial reporting standard. Standards in this area have been adopted by the American Academy of Actuaries and will be further considered by the Actuarial Standards Board.

Extensions of Chapter VII may give rise to standards as to what classification variables, what selection criteria, and what measures controlling antiselection, are to be considered appropriate.

Standards with respect to the degree of conservatism appropriate for some specific actuarial use are obvious extensions of Chapter VIII.

A Case of Apparent Conflict

Chapter IV indicates that the time value of money is an important economic concept, widely used by actuaries and others, and certainly one of the foundations of actuarial science. The Generalized Individual Model of Chapter V includes the factor $(1+i)^{-t}$ in the computation of the expected value of cash flows (in either direction), further indicating the importance that actuaries place upon the "discount for interest."

On the other hand, the principle of conservatism applied to the balance sheet of an insurance enterprise calls for conservative reserves. An important reserve for all insurers, but for property/casualty and health insurers especially, is the liability for incurred but unpaid claims, reported and unreported. One way to make such reserves conservative is to ignore the time value of money (or, what is mathematically the same thing, assume a 0% interest rate).

This conflict between the time value of money and the need for conservatism in the balance sheet of an insurance enterprise was long ago resolved in favor of the latter, so claim reserves are very commonly computed without an interest discount. This treatment makes relatively little difference for those coverages (including life) where claims are paid soon after they are incurred, but, for coverages with "long tails," the differences are significant. If actuaries were free to choose, they might prefer to introduce a discount for interest in the calculation of claim reserves, but the financial statements required by the regulators effectively bar the present value approach for statutory statement purposes.

Consistent with non-recognition of interest in the calculation of claim or loss reserves, the Generalized Individual Model applied to property/casualty coverages commonly ignores the interest discount in the calculation of rates. An important effect of leaving interest out of the basic model is that underwriting gains or losses are separated from investment gains, and that the "bottom line" of a casualty insurance enterprise is shown in two parts—a gain (or loss) from underwriting and a gain from investments. The life company statement combines these into a gain (loss) from operations.

It is the basic premise behind this monograph that actuarial science is one discipline, and that what appear to be life and casualty branches of actuarial endeavor are essentially the same. One distinction between life and casualty actuaries seems to lie in the handling of the time value of money. Life actuaries use a discount for interest as they apply the individual model, whereas casualty actuaries appear to ignore interest in its property/casualty applications.

Appearances are deceiving, however. Casualty actuaries are well aware of the time value of money, and clearly take it into account, albeit somewhat differently. That the financial statement required of U.S. casualty companies has a distinctive treatment of the interest element is a matter of history and tradition, and may make a difference in the way that life and casualty actuaries look at some matters; but it is not an indication that actuarial science has two irreconcilable branches.

Conflicts between Foundations and the Views of the Public

The foundations of actuarial science are not so esoteric or so abstruse that the average well-informed business person has great difficulty in understanding them. There are, however, points at which the actuarial view and that of the general public can come into conflict. Actuaries will do well to recognize where these potential trouble spots are, and to do what they can to resolve misunderstandings.

At the time this monograph is being written, many of the differences between public and actuarial perception revolve around the classification problem. Actuaries are committed to the principle of homogeneous underwriting groups, and are inclined to use any classification variable that has solid statistical significance. The public, and some of those who regulate financial security plans, tend to be wary of "discrimination" of any kind, even though, from the viewpoint of actuaries, the principle of homogeneity promotes equity rather than destroys it.

Questions of financial security system design are often another point of potential conflict. The actuary may be confronted with difficult questions of what benefits to provide and why. Especially in the area of social insurance and employee benefit plans the provisions are complicated, and the rationale unclear. That the actuary is only one of the actors in the design of financial security systems, and in their pricing, is a fact not always understood. Whenever financial security systems run into public disapproval, the actuary, associated as he is with these systems, will feel the pressure.

There may be situations where laws or regulations seem to violate a fundamental actuarial concept. In the United States, the federal regulation of defined benefit pension plans seems to require that the actuary base his actuarial assumptions on "best estimates," whereas many actuaries, in accordance with the principles of Chapter VIII, prefer to introduce an element of conservatism. The problem here is not so much a conflict between actuarial foundations and the regulatory system as it is a contest between two conflicting objectives of the U.S. government. Conservative actuarial assumptions add to the security of employee expectations, and hence promote a basic governmental objective; but conservative assumptions also justify higher corporate income tax deductions, thereby eroding the income tax base, and hence are in conflict with another government purpose. Until the government can resolve this dichotomy, the pension actuary is likely to be "caught in the middle."

Summary

Actuarial standards must ultimately be firmly based on the fundamental concepts of actuarial science, though they may be more directly related to actuarial principles derived from fundamental concepts.

Conflicts may arise when two fundamental concepts appear to be in opposition, or when actuarial concepts appear to conflict with strongly held positions of other disciplines, or the general public.

An understanding of the intellectual underpinnings of these fundamental concepts will enable actuaries to resolve any apparent misunderstandings.